92
Aar

May, Julian

Hank Aaron clinches the pennant

DATE DUE

FEB 8 2000	
APR 2 4 2000	

HANK AARON
CLINCHES THE PENNANT

HANK AARON
CLINCHES THE PENNANT

by Julian May

Published by Crestwood House, Inc., Mankato, Minnesota 56001. Published simultaneously in Canada by J. M. Dent and Sons, Ltd. Library of Congress Catalog Card Number: 72-77304. Standard Book Number: 87191-203-1. Text copyright ©️ 1972 by Julian May Dikty. Illustrations copyright ©️ 1972 by Crestwood House, Inc. All rights reserved. No part of this book may be reproduced in any form without written permission from the publisher, except for brief passages included in a review. Printed in the United States of America.

Designed by William Dichtl

Crestwood House, Inc., Mankato, Minn. 56001

PHOTOGRAPHIC CREDITS

Atlanta Braves: 2, 46; Eau Claire Leader-Telegram: 16; Algimantas Kezys, S.J.: 8; Jerry Sloan: 8-9, 10; United Press International: 6, 9, 12, 13, 14, 15, 18, 19, 20, 21, 22, 23, 25, 26, 27, 28, 29, 31, 32-33, 35, 36, 37, 38, 40, 41, 42, 43, 44, 45, 47; Wide World Photos: 17, 30, 34, 39. Cover: United Press International.

Umpire Shag Crawford calls Hank safe as a Cardinal catcher misses the tag.

HANK AARON
CLINCHES THE PENNANT

Storm clouds rolled in from the Gulf of Mexico. They piled up in black wads over the softball diamond in Mobile, Alabama. In a few minutes, those clouds would zip open and dump game-drowning rain on the team below.

The crowd on the rickety bleachers wasn't looking at the sky. They were watching Henry Aaron, a slender 14-year-old boy.

"Do it, Hank!" somebody yelled. Thunder rumbled.

It was the last of the ninth. The team was behind, 3-1. There was a man on first, and one on third, with two outs.

The boy in the batter's box stood quietly. He gripped the bat in a strange way. A righthander, he had his left hand on top in a cross-handed grip.

The first pitch was wide of the plate—a sure ball. But Hank didn't want to wait. He was thinking: "If it starts to pour, they might call the game. We'd lose."

He waded into the bad pitch.

Splat! The softball blasted off into the farthest reaches of the outfield. It was getting dark. The outfielder lost the ball.

The fans screamed as Hank's two team-mates scored. Then Hank himself came sliding home through the dust, and the game was won.

Friends pounded Hank on the back. Some of the team were jumping up and down with joy. But Hank just gave a little smile and started picking up his things to go home.

"Hey, man," one boy said to him. "Don't you even *care?*"

"There's just one thing I care about now," Hank replied. "And that's what's going to happen to me when my mother sees these dirty pants."

The team broke up laughing. That Hank. He always had a wise answer.

He was a boy who was hard to know. Even though he was the best sandlot slugger in all Mobile, he had few close friends. Many of the black boys in his neighborhood formed into gangs. But Henry Aaron was different. He spent a lot of time at the library and at home.

He learned fairly early that the other boys admired his hitting, but were uneasy about his brains. So he was quiet around the dugout. Some of the big mouths on the team said he spent most of his time asleep. "He only wakes up when the pitch comes in," they laughed.

Nobody laughed at his batting average, though. One season, it was .700 . . . and Hank was the team's workhorse hitter.

His father was a shipyard welder. The family lived in a neat frame house in the Toulminville neighborhood of Mobile. It was a nice place, far better than many of the other black sections of the city.

Some boys on the other teams envied and hated the kids from Toulminville. Sometimes there were fights.

Hank himself never got into trouble. But the idea of black fighting black made him unhappy. One day he said to his father:

"I can sort of understand how black and white people find it hard to get along. But these kids from Down the Bay—why, they really think they're *blacker* than us. Just because they live in a worse place!"

"It's like a boy who can't afford candy," said his father. "He might tell himself it's no good anyway."

But it was a long time before Hank understood.

Mobile, Alabama, the gulfport city that was Hank Aaron's early home. In the background are the docks where ocean-going ships tie up.

Hank's boyhood hero, Jackie Robinson, pulls down a high throw in 1947, at the start of his major-league career. Robinson was National League batting champion and Most Valuable Player in 1949. He retired in 1956 and was elected to Baseball's Hall of Fame.

Black hatred cost Hank his first chance at a big-league tryout. A Dodgers scout came to Mobile when the boy was 15 and a top player on the semi-pro Black Bears team.

The Dodgers had always been a "hero team" to Hank. Hadn't they hired Jackie Robinson, the first black man to play in the major leagues? He went eagerly to the tryout.

Hank was a good shortstop. But when it came time for his turn at fielding, a big boy from Down the Bay shoved him aside and took his place. There were threats, ugly words.

Hank wouldn't fight. It wasn't his way. So he just picked up and left.

All through high school Hank continued to play baseball. He played football, too, and was good at it. But a career on the diamond remained the boy's secret hope. He didn't talk about it with his parents, because they wanted him to go to college.

In 1951, when Hank was 17, a scout from the Negro American League saw him play. "I'd like to hire you, kid," the scout said. "We'll pay $200 a month." It seemed like a lot of money to Hank.

But his parents refused to let him go. Hank pleaded with them. He tried to make them understand how much baseball meant to him. The Negro League scout talked to Mr. and Mrs. Aaron, too. He told them it was possible for Hank to become a truly great player.

Finally, Mr. and Mrs. Aaron gave in. Hank must finish high school. Then he could join the team.

The next spring, Hank signed a contract with the Indianapolis Clowns, one of the top teams in the league. He took a train to the Clowns camp in South Carolina and arrived full of hope and nearly scared to death.

Being frightened didn't hurt his game. The first time out, he went 10 for 11 at the plate. Playing shortstop, he started five double plays.

There were major league scouts at the Clowns camp. They said to themselves, "What have we here?"

Young Henry Aaron in Milwaukee Braves uniform.

They found out soon enough. Off the field, Hank was shy, full of self-doubt. He took a nap whenever he had a chance. And he still batted in that crazy cross-handed way whenever he thought the coaches weren't looking.

But by May, his batting average was .467.

Five major league teams tried to buy him from the Clowns. Hank finally had to choose between the New York Giants and the Milwaukee Braves. He took the Braves. They sent him to their Class C team in Eau Claire, Wisconsin.

Two weeks after he arrived, he was selected as shortstop for the All-Star Team.

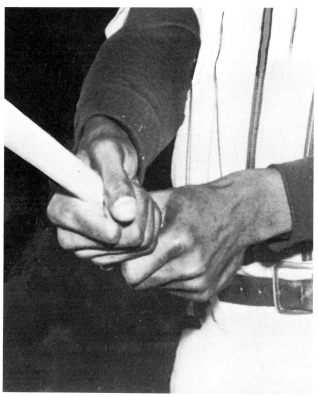
Hank's powerful grip

He showed them his special style—hitting almost every kind of pitch that sailed his way. His mighty wrists whipped the bat around. It connected—and another screaming line drive would go on its way. The ball was so hot that fielders often couldn't keep it. Hank made many bases on their errors.

He finished that season as league rookie of the year. But he was lonely in Eau Claire. People tried to be friendly—but he was almost the only black man in town. He felt strange and homesick for the South.

17

The manager of the Jacksonville Tars, Ben Geraghty, talks with his star second baseman, Henry Aaron, in 1953.

Next season he moved up to the Class A Jacksonville Tars. This Florida city had never known Negro ballplayers in its league. Hank and his team-mate, Felix Mantilla, were the first. In those days, many places in the South had laws that kept black people out of the best restaurants and hotels. Hank and Felix were sometimes booed.

Strangely enough, Hank didn't mind. This was the world he was used to. He ignored the insults and just played ball.

The Jacksonville manager was Ben Geraghty. Years later, Hank called Ben the best manager he'd ever played for. Ben cured Hank of his bad batting habits and helped him to grow in confidence.

When Hank made mistakes, Ben was usually patient. But one day, Hank was in a base-stealing mood. He stole second three times. Each time, he stepped off the bag while the baseman still had the ball. Each time he was tagged.

Ben exploded. "Once is forgivable," the manager said. "Twice is dumb. But *three times is ridiculous!*"

Hank was never caught off-base again.

Hank is tagged out.

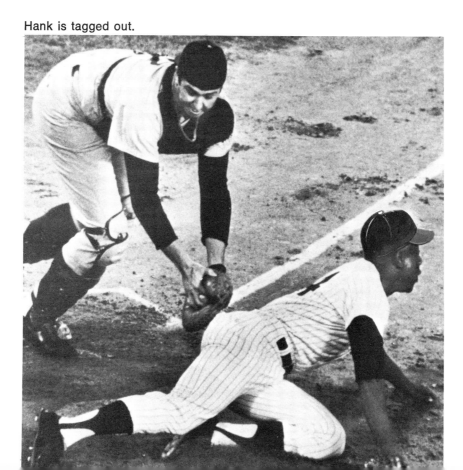

Early in the season, Hank met a pretty girl named Barbara ·Lucas. They fell in love. But Barbara's parents didn't think much of Hank. How many minor-league ball players ever became really successful?

Hank waited. He finished the season leading the league in runs, hits, runs batted in, two-baggers, put-outs, and assists. His batting average was .362, tops in the league, He was voted Most Valuable Player.

"Now will you marry me, Barbara?" he asked.

Her parents decided that Hank might amount to something after all. They gave their approval. Hank and Barbara were married in the fall of 1953.

Hank and his wife, Barbara

Hank was already a big-league hitter. But he had made 36 errors playing second base in 1953—another minor-league record. They switched him to the outfield and had him work through the winter in the Puerto Rican League. It looked as though he would go to Toledo, a Class AAA club, in spring.

Then Braves' outfielder Bobby Thomson broke his ankle in an exhibition game. Without any fanfare, Hank Aaron was put on the roster of the Milwaukee team.

Nobody knew much about him except manager Charlie Grimm. After his first game, with no hits in five at-bats, Hank felt very low.

"You're just a little scared, kid," said Charlie Grimm. "Loosen up, and everything will be fine."

Early in 1954, Manager Charlie Grimm *(left)* had his eye on young Hank Aaron. Here Grimm congratulates Hank after a homer during a game in spring training.

Hank scores the winning run in a game against the New York Giants.

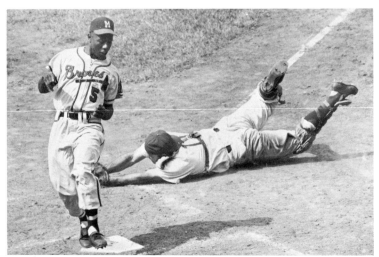

Too late, Chicago Cubs' catcher Joe Garagiola dives for the ball as Hank comes home. This game was in August 1954.

Curve balls from big-league pitchers were hard for Hank to handle at first. Charlie Grimm had him practice with Braves' hurlers Lew Burdette and Warren Spahn. Hank's game improved. He hit his first home run on April 23, 1954. After that, he knew he would make it in the big leagues.

Saying very little, he worked hard on his batting and fielding. He made many mistakes, but learned from them. Once he slid into third when there was already a man on base. Another time he failed to score because his cap fell off and he went back to pick it up.

But there were other days, too, when his batting helped win ball games. The Braves were aiming for a pennant, and Hank Aaron was going to help them get it.

22

In early September, the Braves played a double-header in Cincinnati. During the second game, Hank came to bat in the ninth, with the team leading 9-7.

He smacked the ball deep into center field and began running. It looked like a sure triple. As the ball came whistling toward third, Hank slid in.

He caught his spikes in the bag and broke his ankle. Gloom settled over the team. They had lost their great rookie for the rest of the season. It was the end of the Milwaukee pennant fever. The team came in third.

Hank shows his ankle in a cast.

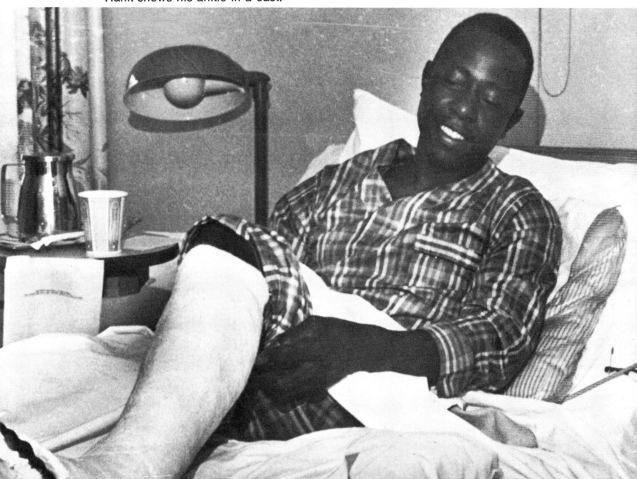

No city had ever wanted a pennant as much as Milwaukee. Big-league baseball had come to town for the first time in 1953. The fans made instant heroes out of their team. They flocked to the home games and rooted so hard that visiting teams were amazed and a little envious.

The Braves responded by playing hard and well. They had come in second in the National League three times. Many felt the team was overdue for a pennant.

By spring, 1955, Hank's broken ankle was healed and as good as ever. He was ready for a great year.

The batting stance of Hank Aaron

Wes Westrum, Giant catcher, reaches in vain for a peg from Willie Mays. Hank scored a winning run by a split second in this game, July 17, 1955, and the Braves won 8-7.

He was only 21 years old, and already one of the most feared bats in the league. Pitchers tried every kind of ball on him. He seemed to hit them all, bad as well as good.

He often held the bat in a careless way. Once he had the label turned toward the pitcher. Someone told him he should turn it so he could read the label.

"But, man," said Hank, "I didn't come here to read."

That year he batted .314 and tied for the league lead in two-base hits. He topped the Braves lineup in batting, hits, and runs batted in.

The Braves were second in 1955, but still as pennant-hungry as ever. Hank started the next season in a slump and didn't break out until the All-Star Game. After that, he had a fine 25-game hitting streak that racked up 44 hits. The Milwaukee team stayed hot for the rest of the summer. By September, they led the league.

But the Brooklyn Dodgers slowly crept up on them. On the next-to-last day of the season, the Bums inched ahead by half a game. The Braves had to win their next game with St. Louis in order to tie.

A frantic lunge failed to net Hank the ball in this game against the Giants in 1956.

It was a night game. The Braves had Warren Spahn on the mound, a great southpaw hurler. The Cardinal's pitcher was Herman Wehmeier. A hit by Hank in the first inning drove in a run for the Braves. The Cardinals scored in the sixth. Then it became a heart-stopping pitchers' duel.

The score remained tied into the twelfth inning, when Stan Musial finally wrapped up the game for St. Louis, 2-1.

The Braves had only one more game to play. They won. So did the Dodgers—and there went the pennant. But Hank was National League batting champion in 1956 with an average of .328. He also led the league with 200 hits.

National League President Warren Giles presents Hank with a silver bat, emblem of the league batting title.

Hank poses with his baby son, Henry Aaron, Jr.

Now that he was a top baseball star, sports writers flocked around him. They wanted to know all about him.

But Hank had always been quiet and thoughtful. He didn't want to talk about himself. If writers pushed him, Hank sometimes made up stories for them.

He told them that Stan Musial helped him develop his batting style. But the great St. Louis slugger hardly knew Hank. The Aaron batting style was Hank's very own. But he was too modest to admit it.

The great hands and wrists of Hank Aaron were not really developed by youthful exercise. He was born with powerful muscles, and learned how to use his natural gifts.

Another time, a writer asked, "How did you develop those great wrists?"

"Delivering tons and tons of ice down in Mobile," said Hank. But it was only a joke. He was born with the wrists.

For four years, the Braves had come close to the pennant, only to lose it. They were determined to win in 1957. But it wouldn't be easy. The Dodgers, the Cards, and the Cincinnati Reds were all in contention.

Hank did his part. From June to August, the Braves were in second place. In mid-month, they climbed to first. Then came a slump, but Hank helped the team pull out. By the end of September, Milwaukee was leading again.

They met the St. Louis Cardinals on September 23 for the deciding game.

Batting against the Dodgers in 1957, Hank lets loose with what looks like a one-handed smash.

It was almost a repeat of the last year's squeaker. The score was tied at 2-2 in the eleventh inning. With one out and one man on, Hank stepped up to the plate. The fans were screaming at him, begging for the hit that would give Milwaukee the league championship.

Umpire Shag Crawford calls Hank safe as a Cardinal catcher misses the tag.

Hank stood at the plate, eyes half closed, body relaxed. You might have thought he was asleep—unless you knew Hank Aaron. The ball hurtled toward him and he waited. Waited. It had almost reached the catcher's mitt before Hank swung.

Wood met leather and the ball arched upward. It was a home run. Hank had clinched the first Milwaukee pennant.

Jubilant team-mates carry Hank from the field after his pennant-winning home run. At left, Andy Pafko; second from left, Gene Conley.

Now Hank Aaron was the shining hero of thousands of sports fans all over the upper midwest. A few weeks earlier, he had moved his wife and their four young children from Mobile to Milwaukee. The winning city was now their home. They could share whole-heartedly in the victory.

Hank and Mickey Mantle of the New York Yankees posed together before the start of the 1957 World Series. Mantle was one of the all-time sluggers, named Most Valuable Player in 1956, 1957, and 1962.

For the World Series, the Braves were pitted against the powerful New York Yankees, who were thought to be unbeatable. But the contest see-sawed back and forth, with the Braves winning every other game. Tied at three games apiece, the teams met for the final battle in Yankee Stadium.

Hank hits a home run during the fourth game of the 1957 World Series.

Fellow Braves congratulate Hank as he trots around the bases. His three-run homer helped seal a 7-5 Braves victory.

The National League Most Valuable Player award for 1957 went to Hank Aaron. Braves pitcher Warren Spahn won the Cy Young Award for Most Valuable Pitcher.

It was a beautiful game, the frosting on Milwaukee's cake. Lew Burdette pitched a 5-0 shutout. The New York fans gave him a splendid hand. They were disappointed that the Yankees had lost the Series, but they admired the spirit of the underdog Braves who had won in spite of long odds.

Hank shared top honors with Lew Burdette. He had hit 3 homers, batted in 7 runs, and slugged an average of .393, better than any other Series player. He finished the season leading the league in runs, in home runs, and in runs batted in. He won the Most Valuable Player award for 1957.

The sixth game of the 1958 World Series featured this collision at first base between Hank and Yankee first baseman Moose Skowron. A throw from the pitcher on Aaron's bunt hit Hank on the shoulder. Another Braves runner made second on the error.

People began to speak of Hank as a "superstar." He helped his team to a second pennant in 1958. But the Yankees won the 1958 World Series, four games to three.

During the years that followed, Hank's playing stayed sensational—while his private life was very quiet. He and Barbara raised their children. They also studied so that they could enter the real estate business. Both of them knew that an athlete's career does not last forever. They wanted to be prepared for later life.

Young fans ask Hank for his autograph.

Despite his shyness, Hank wanted to help children. So without telling anyone, he would visit hospitals and homes for the retarded. There he talked to the children and even taught them to play ball. It made the kids happy, and it filled Hank with a quiet joy, too.

40

The baseball fans of Milwaukee had less reason
to cheer. The Braves came in second in 1959, losing
the play-off to the Los Angeles Dodgers. Hank took
the batting title that year with an average of .355.

Hank starts along the base path after slamming a good one in 1959.

In 1960, the city of Milwaukee seemed to lose some of its love for its baseball team. The Braves came in second, but fewer fans attended the games. The team was like a toy that was growing old. Morale suffered.

The 1961 season did not look promising. Older players were retiring or being let go. Fielding was weak, and Hank found himself shuffled around from position to position as the manager tried to find a winning combination.

It was a forlorn hope. The team came in fourth.

Hank steals third in a 1961 game against the Los Angeles Dodgers.

Hank's brother, Tommie Aaron *(right),* joined the Braves in 1962. He played for both the Milwaukee and Atlanta ball clubs.

The Braves dropped to fifth in 1962. Hank was still tops; but one superstar isn't a winning ball club.

During the 1963 season, Hank came close to taking the Triple Crown. He led the league with 130 runs batted in, tied for home-run champ with 44. But his final batting average was .319, 7 points below Los Angeles' Tommy Davis.

The Braves were sixth. The owners were thinking of moving the team to Atlanta, Georgia.

Hank had mixed feelings about the switch. The warm climate would help his second son, Larry, who suffered from asthma. But Hank did not want his family to face the prejudice that was so common in the South.

The Braves finally went to Atlanta in 1966. Hank's doubts proved to be unfounded. The Aarons moved to a beautiful house in a neighborhood having both black and white families. Atlanta turned out to be a friendly city that supported its new team—even when the Braves were less than champs.

Hank kept on slugging. In 1969 he was appointed team captain. On May 17, 1970, he got his 3,000th base hit. Only nine other players in history have passed this mark.

As newly appointed team captain, Hank "inspects" team-mates Ken Johnson, Tito Francona, and Bob Tillman.

The only living baseball players to attain 3,000 hits in their careers posed together in 1971. From left to right: Stan Musial, Willie Mays, Henry Aaron. Musial made the 3,000 mark in 1958. Mays and Aaron reached the magic number in 1970.

On April 27, 1971, Hank Aaron hit his 600th home run. Both Hank and Willie Mays threaten the all-time 714 home run record of Babe Ruth.

Modest as ever, Hank Aaron seldom made the headlines. But when he did, it was for a good reason. In 1971, he slammed out his 600th home run. Babe Ruth's all-time record was 714. But Hank refused to say whether he thought he could top it.

"One home run is the same as another," he said, smiling.

Millions of baseball fans wouldn't agree. They sent Hank's ball and bat to Baseball's Hall of Fame. And Hank's own place among the greatest hitters of all time is secure.

In early 1972, Hank smiles as he signs a three-year contract for $600,000, making him the highest-paid player in baseball history.

HENRY LOUIS AARON

He was born February 5, 1934, at Mobile, Alabama, the son of Herbert and Estella Aaron. He attended Central High and a private school, Josephine Allen Institute. When he was 15, he began to play with the semipro Black Bears. After graduation, he joined the Indianapolis Clowns of the Negro American League, but played for only a short time before his contract was purchased by the Milwaukee Braves.

From May until September, 1952, he played with the Class C Eau Claire club of the Braves' farm system. He spent the 1953 season with Jacksonville, a Class A team.

He married Barbara Lucas on October 6, 1953. The couple have four children——Henry, Jr., Larry, Gail, and Dorinda. From 1954 through 1965 he played for the Milwaukee Braves. Since 1966 he has played for the Atlanta Braves.

HENRY AARON STATISTICS

Year	Club	G	AB	R	H	2B	3B	HR	RBI	BA
1952	Eau Claire	87	345	79	116	19	4	9	61	.336
1953	Jacksonville	137	574	*115	*208	*36	14	22	*125	*.362
1954	Milwaukee	122	468	58	131	27	6	13	69	.280
1955	Milwaukee	153	602	105	189	**37	9	27	106	.314
1956	Milwaukee	153	609	106	*200	*34	14	26	92	*.328
1957	Milwaukee	151	615	*118	198	27	6	*44	*132	.322
1958	Milwaukee	153	601	109	196	34	4	30	95	.326
1959	Milwaukee	154	629	116	*223	46	7	39	123	*.355
1960	Milwaukee	153	590	102	172	20	11	40	*126	.292
1961	Milwaukee	155	603	115	197	*39	10	34	120	.327
1962	Milwaukee	156	592	127	191	28	6	45	128	.323
1963	Milwaukee	161	631	*121	201	29	4	**44	*130	.319
1964	Milwaukee	145	570	103	187	30	2	24	95	.328
1965	Milwaukee	150	570	109	181	*40	1	32	89	.318
1966	Atlanta	158	603	117	168	23	1	*44	*127	.279
1967	Atlanta	155	600	**113	184	37	3	*39	109	.307
1968	Atlanta	160	606	84	174	33	4	29	86	.287
1969	Atlanta	147	547	100	164	30	3	44	97	.300
1970	Atlanta	150	516	103	154	26	1	38	118	.298
1971	Atlanta	139	495	95	162	22	3	47	118	.327
	M.L. Totals	2715	10447	1901	3272	562	95	639	1960	.313

* League leader
** Tied league leader

Most Valuable Player: 1957

CONCORD OXBOW SCHOOL